Silly Squirrel

Activity Book

T0346980

Name _____

Age _____

Class _____

OXFORD
UNIVERSITY PRESS

OXFORD
UNIVERSITY PRESS

Great Clarendon Street, Oxford OX2 6DP

Oxford University Press is a department of the University of Oxford.
It furthers the University's objective of excellence in research, scholarship,
and education by publishing worldwide in

Oxford New York

Auckland Bangkok Buenos Aires Cape Town Chennai
Dar es Salaam Delhi Hong Kong Istanbul Karachi Kolkata
Kuala Lumpur Madrid Melbourne Mexico City Mumbai
Nairobi São Paulo Shanghai Taipei Tokyo Toronto

OXFORD and OXFORD ENGLISH are registered trade marks of
Oxford University Press in the UK and in certain other countries

ISBN 13: 978 0 19 440136 4

ISBN 10: 0 19 440136 7

Printed in China

Activities by: Rebecca Brooke
Illustrations by: Ingela Peterson
Original story by: Craig Wright

Connect.

apple •

banana •

lemon •

orange •

egg •

sandwich •

Circle.

❶ two squirrels

❷ one squirrel

❸ four squirrels

❹ three squirrels

Circle.

1 Sid is hungry.

2 Sid is cold.

3 Sid is hot.

4 Sid is happy.

Write.

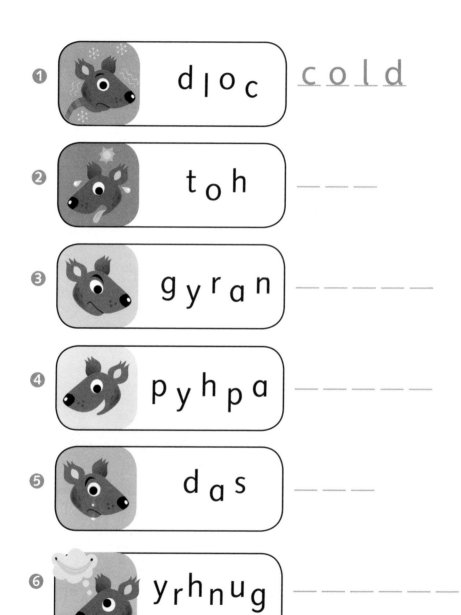

1. d l o c   <u>c o l d</u>
2. t o h
3. g y r a n
4. p y h p a
5. d a s
6. y r h n u g

Chant.

Can you see a squirrel?

　Yes, I can.

Can you see a bird?

　Yes, I can.

Can you see a banana?

　Yes, I can.

Can you see an orange?

　Yes, I can.

Can you see an apple?

　Yes, I can.

Can you see a lemon?

　Yes, I can.

Write.

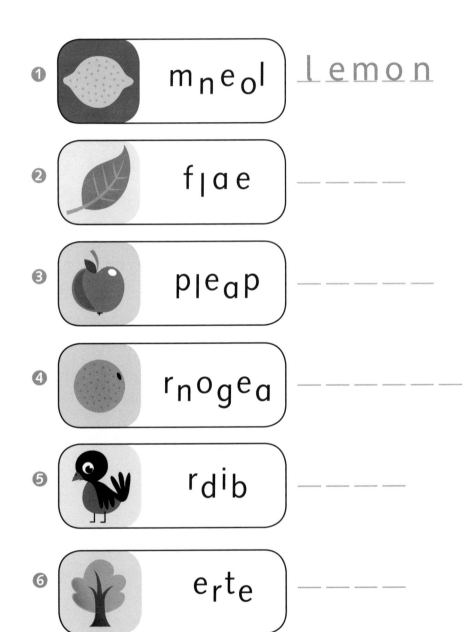

1. m n e o l   l e m o n

2. f l a e   _ _ _ _ _

3. p l e a p   _ _ _ _ _

4. r n o g e a   _ _ _ _ _ _

5. r d i b   _ _ _ _

6. e r t e   _ _ _ _

Write.

> red   green   yellow
> brown   white

① The banana is ___yellow___ .

② The apple is _____ .

③ The egg is _____ .

④ The leaf is _____ .

⑤ The lemon is _____ .

⑥ Sid is _____ .

Circle.

1. Sid is a...
   bird (squirrel) tree

2. Sid is in a...
   leaf   squirrel   tree

3. Sid is...   hot   cold   angry

4. Sid is...   hungry   sad   hot

5. Sid is looking for...
   a tree   a bird   food

6. Sid has a...
   bird   leaf   lemon

Chant.

Winter is here.

Sid is cold.

Winter is here.

Sid is hungry.

Sid looks for food.

He finds an apple.

Sid looks for food.

He finds a lemon, too.

Sid looks for food.

He finds a banana.

Sid looks for food.

He finds an orange, too.

Write.

> orange   looks   squirrel
> finds   hungry   here

❶ Sid is a ___squirrel___ .

❷ Sid _____ a banana.

❸ Sid _____ for food.

❹ Winter is _____ .

❺ Sid finds an _____ .

❻ Sid is _____ .

Connect.

Sid finds a banana.

Sid finds an egg.

Sid has an apple.

Sid is a squirrel.

Sid looks for food.

Winter is here.

Circle yes **or** no .

1. Can you see a banana?

   yes no

2. Can you see an orange?

   yes no

3. Can you see a sandwich?

   yes no

4. Can you see an egg?

   yes no

5. Can you see an apple?

   yes no

6. Can you see a leaf?

   yes no

Circle yes **or** no .

1. Sid is a bird.   yes (no)

2. It is winter.   yes no

3. Winter is hot.   yes no

4. Sid is hot.   yes no

5. Sid is cold.   yes no

6. Sid is hungry.   yes no

7. Sid finds a banana.   yes no

8. Sid is a silly squirrel.   yes no

Look and write.

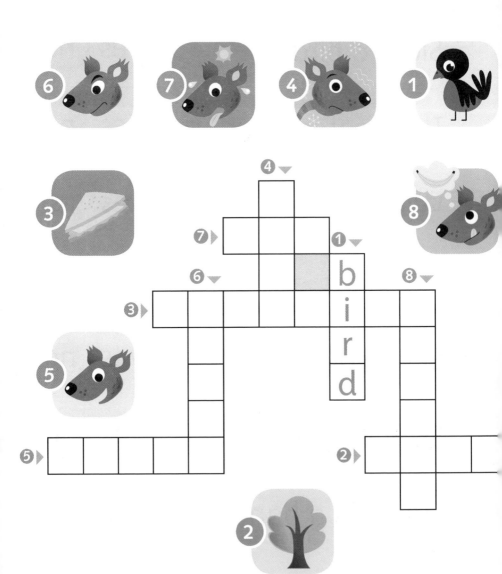